Struggle to Survive

Struggle to Survive

ROBERT D. STREET

ISBN-13: 9781519792488
ISBN-10: 1519792484

Dedication

*T*his book is dedicated to everyone who has served in the armed forces of our country, from the eighteenth-century minutemen to the valiant troops who serve today. It is especially dedicated to the valorous thousands who were forced to endure the infamous Bataan Death March. May God bless you and hold you in the palm of his hand.

Acknowledgments

I wish to acknowledge a longtime friend, Clara Strickland, for the invaluable assistance she gave by proof-reading as I completed this biography of John Leroy Mims. She and I were colleagues at Richmond Community College in Hamlet, North Carolina, for many years. Thanks, Clara.

Table of Contents

One

John Leroy Mims was born on November 25, 1922, in Ashburn, Georgia, to his Native American parents, Robert "Bob" Mims and Annie Railey Mims. He had an older brother, Joseph L. Mims, who was in the US Army in Europe during World War II. He also had a half brother, Robert, and a half sister, Louise.

About three months after John was born, his mother died from blood poisoning. Soon thereafter his father took three-month-old John and his older brother, Joseph, to the Indian reservation. It was located in in the Florida Panhandle near the community of Bonifay, which is about 125 miles east of Pensacola. John and Joseph spent several years there with both of their grandmothers, who cared for them and other children.

John & Joseph Mims 1927

His grandmothers lived in a large house with an extra-wide fireplace, over which they cooked the family meals. A couple of vertical iron bars with arms stood on each side of the fireplace.

A wide porch surrounded the house on three sides, and the children spent many happy hours playing there and in the huge yard. The yard was covered with sand and had a few scraggly bushes as well as palmetto bushes, pines, a few water oaks, and the occasional cypress tree growing close to nearby streams. There was plenty of space for the children to play hide-and-seek and other childhood games.

A family garden behind the house contained a wide assortment of vegetables, including tomatoes, potatoes, peas, squash, green beans, lettuce, and cabbage. Watermelons and cantaloupes were a special treat that were greatly appreciated by young and old alike. Blackberries grew along a fence made of saplings, which were interlaced for strength to keep varmints from razing the garden.

During the summer, most of the vegetables not eaten by the family were canned for winter consumption. Many hands helped the grandmothers prepare the vegetables for canning, as aunts, uncles, and cousins all pitched in to help put up food for the coming winter. Any food not eaten or canned was available for sale to the public in the two stores Mr. Mims owned.

After he learned to walk, John loved to follow the bigger kids wherever they went. When they entered the forest, they taught John to walk softly and quietly so as not to scare the animals. John learned that the older kids were good at hunting and fishing, and they taught him many useful outdoor skills as he grew older. They hunted deer, rabbits, squirrels, and hogs. Whenever they killed an animal, they removed the entrails before taking it back to the reservation for the grandmothers to process and cook.

Sometimes the boys would catch a live hog, using hounds and coonhounds. When they caught one, they would take it to Uncle Charlie Pitt's farm, where it was put in a strong pen built of logs placed horizontally and only inches apart.

John enjoyed each hunting trip he made with the other boys. He said of those days, "Skills I learned then served me well during combat and when I was a prisoner of war."

One of John's favorite recollections as a child growing up on the reservation was getting to go fishing with his uncles and other children in the village. John said, "We ate a lot of fish, which we caught in streams near the village. When we went down to the streams where we fished, we could easily see the fish because the water was crystal clear." He continued, "We used a three-pronged gig. Each prong had a barb to hold the fish."

As a Native American youngster, John was different in appearance from the other kids on the reservation. He had blond hair and blue eyes. The other children had black hair and dark eyes. This different appearance caused some hardship for John as the other children pulled at his blond hair. They thought they could put it on their heads so they, too, would have blond hair.

The harassment became so severe and frequent that his grandmothers finally told John to stay on the porch and forbade the other children to come up on the porch. He had another advantage too: Joseph, his older brother, became John's protector whenever the children began to tease him. The teasing soon stopped.

John loved being on the reservation, and he loved his surroundings. He described them, saying, "We were in a beautiful location. The trees were tall and gracious, the streams were clear and beautiful, and it was a wonderful place for a child to grow up."

John's father married again a few years after John was taken to the reservation. Soon after, he came to get John and Joseph and took them home to their step-mother. John said of her, "She was a hard disciplinarian, and we were crossways with her for a long time. But eventually things smoothed out, and our relationship with her improved."

For years after Mr. Mims took John and Joseph back to his home after he remarried, the boys continued to spend time with their grandmothers and others on the reservation, especially during the summer months.

Mr. Mims owned a farm of several hundred acres as well as two country stores. He worked for the railroad, hauling crossties from the forest, and on the side, he ran a prosperous moonshine business. John and Joseph were heavily involved in the moonshine business, even as young boys. Two ladies ran the stores, keeping the records, buying replacement stock, and handling sales in the stores. Mr. Mims also had a foreman who ran the ranch.

John recalled that there were animals of all kinds on the farm. He listed chickens, turkeys, hogs, cows, horses, goats, dogs, and cats. Most of the animals roamed free.

Having been born in 1922, John was just a young lad of almost seven when the great stock market crash occurred in 1929. In the years leading up to that event, events had begun to go badly for Mr. Mims. John said he could remember hearing conversations in one of his father's stores similar to this between Mr. Mims and a customer: "Mr. Mims, I ain't got nothing at home to feed my family, and I ain't got no money. If you'll let me have some food on credit, I'll pay you as soon as I get some." Unfortunately the customer was unable to get any money with which to pay Mr. Mims before Mr. Mims lost both of his stores and the farm.

But that was not the only problem John's father had. Leading up to the time before the crash, Mr. Mims had been making, hauling, and selling moonshine liquor. During those hard economic times, money was hard to come by. There was little work by which one could earn money. Even though people had little money, it seemed they could always find enough to buy some liquor, and Mr. Mims was there to fill that need.

When John was just six years old, he and Joseph were actively involved in their father's moonshine business. John had a small wagon on which he would load pints and half-pints of moonshine, pulling the wagon around the farm and hiding the jars.

John said, "I had a good memory, and I could easily remember where I had hidden both the pints and half-pints, and I could quickly get a jar of liquor for a customer and take his money." His father had told

John and Joseph that if the law caught Mr. Mims selling the liquor, he would be put in jail, but the law officers would not do anything if they caught the boys selling the liquor. So John and Joseph would hand the liquor to the customer and take the money. A pint of the moonshine sold for a dollar, and a half-pint sold for fifty cents.

John recalled one instance when, while he and his father were making a delivery, they came upon a police barricade. His father pushed the accelerator to the floorboard, and the police backed up their cars so his father could pass safely. He escaped that time, but he was caught later. The police began putting pressure on Mr. Mims. With the cost of lawyers and courts and hardships of the Depression, Mr. Mims's financial situation became more and more precarious. He lost farm and both of his stores.

John's father was arrested, convicted of bootlegging and sentenced to jail. It was indeed a dark and difficult time for the Mims family. John said of those times, "Many times when we went to visit Daddy in jail, we had had nothing to eat, and we were fed in that 'ball-and-chain' facility."

For a short time, when John was only twelve, he worked for an uncle, Charlie Pitt, who owned several hundred acres of land near Youngstown, Florida. John rode a horse as he tended his uncle's cattle.

Mr. Mims sometimes personally enjoyed the product of his labors in the moonshine business. One evening, having made a delivery of the illicit product to a customer in Tallahassee, he began drinking some of the brew and was riding in the bed of the pickup truck on his way home. Another driver ran into the truck head-on, killing Mr. Mims in the accident.

Two

WORK IN THE CCC

When his father was killed in the wreck, John was fifteen years old. Finding himself an orphan for a second time, he ran away from home and joined the Civilian Conservation Corps (CCC), a program begun by the Roosevelt administration to help stimulate the failing economy by putting people to work so they would have money to spend. When he joined the CCC, John thought he was joining the army because soldiers were in charge of the program.

He and others were taken to Fort McPherson near Atlanta, Georgia. When they arrived, the foreman in charge asked the assembled youth, "Who can drive a truck?" John said that just about every boy present raised his hand. The foreman ordered them to follow him up over a rise in the land. When they reached the top of the small hill, they looked down and saw what looked like hundreds of wheelbarrows. The foreman then told them, "We are going to move dirt from here to there, and from there to there." With these instructions, the boys began to move dirt for what would eventually become a golf course.

Work on the golf course continued for several months. When this work was finished, the youths were loaded onto a westbound train. Their destination, they were told, was Camp Applegate in Medford, Oregon. When they reached the Grand Canyon in Arizona, they stopped so all of them could see it. Of this experience, John said, "We were in complete awe at the majesty and scope of the Grand Canyon. None of us had ever seen anything so spectacular and breathtaking. It was absolutely gorgeous."

Following their stop at the Grand Canyon, the CCC youths reboarded the train and continued to their destination in Oregon. When they arrived at Camp Applegate, fires raged through the forest. John said of the fires, "They were so intense that they would crown in the tops of the huge pines and seem to explode as the fire moved from tree to tree. It was something to behold!"

The youths began to help fight the fires, and after several days, when things had settled down, their next job was to cut pine trees for a road that was to be built. Many of the trees they cut down were split into firewood to use to heat their barracks during the coming winter. As winter approached, it was essential that they have fuel to keep the barracks warm. During this process, John was given a higher rank and put in charge of making sure they had cut and stacked enough wood to heat the barracks that winter.

The youngsters were able to go into Medford on Friday nights for dances held in the community. John was among those who attended, where they mingled with the local young people. He met a couple of pretty girls he liked and hung out with, dancing and enjoying their company. At a break in one of the first dances he attended, the young girls, who were sisters, introduced him to their parents. In talking with the parents, John learned that they owned a large ranch nearby.

After the dances were over, they were supposed to meet a truck at 11:00 p.m. to return to the camp, but John purposely missed the truck so he could have more dances with the local beauties. Of course when he returned to the camp, he was late, and as punishment for his tardiness, he was assigned KP duty in the kitchen for a week. Of this John said, "I had to work on KP for several weeks because I was late coming back from the dances, but it was worth it to me to be able to spend that extra time with those cute girls."

One day, as John was engaged in his KP duties, he was assigned the job of washing pots and pans. As he was at work, the pastry cook came in with a pan from which he had just emptied dough for a cake. He set the pan down near John and said, "Here, wash this," and turned to leave. John saw what was in the pan, picked it up, ran his finger around the pan to collect some of the remaining cake dough, tasted it, and said, "Mmmm, boy, this is good!" The cook heard him, turned, jerked the pan out of John's hands, said, "This is for you to wash, not to eat," threw the pan down on the rack with other pots and pans, and turned to leave. Again John picked up the pan, and as before, scraped up some of the cake dough with his finger and put it in his mouth. The cook saw this and approached John, raising his hand as if to hit John. As the cook raised his hand, John saw it, reached out, caught the cook's hand, and pulled the cook over to the rack where the posts and pans were sitting, causing all of them to fall on the cook.

Hearing the commotion in the kitchen, the first sergeant came in, saw what was happening, and told them to take it outside if they were going to fight. The cook went outside first, with John following. As John stepped outside, the cook took a swing at him. John saw the swing coming, sidestepped the blow, hit the cook with his right hand, and knocked him out!

About this time, another supervisor came outside to see what was happening. After seeing what had taken place, he told the first sergeant that maybe they should make a prizefighter out of John. So they set up two fights for him. The first fight was in Rogue River, Oregon, in another CCC camp. John won! But a check of his personnel records revealed that John was too young to be in the CCC, so he was discharged.

Upon being discharged from the CCC, the parents of the girls he had met at the dances in Medford, the Hewitts, offered him a job as a foreman on their ranch outside Medford. He worked hard for the Hewitts and saved most of his earnings. He worked for them for about two years. After just a few months, John realized that he had earned and saved enough money to buy his first car.

Three

On September 16, 1940, President Franklin D. Roosevelt signed the Selective Service and Training Act, which required all male citizens between the ages of twenty-six and thirty-five to register for the military draft beginning on October 16. The act had been passed by Congress ten days earlier.[1]

Two of his friends had received notice that they were being drafted. They were ordered to report for their physical examinations to Vancouver Barracks in Washington State. Since neither man had transportation to the examination, John offered to drive them

---

1 "Sept. 16, 1940, This Day in History: Franklin Roosevelt Approves Military Draft," *Wikipedia*, http://en.wikipedia.org/. (Accessed 11-23-15)

there himself since he was the only one of the three who owned an automobile.

They reported for their examinations at the appointed time. One of them was found to have high blood sugar, and he was ordered to Fort McClellan in Anniston, Alabama, where he was from. The other friend passed the examination and was ordered to California for basic training.

While John had been waiting for his friends to complete their examinations, he sat in the waiting area of the processing center. An old sergeant, whose face identified him as one with years of service and who appeared to have no teeth, approached John and told him he should go to the Philippines. John asked him why, and the sergeant told him that the Filipinos loved blond hair and blue eyes.

At that time, John was eighteen years of age and old enough to join the army. He was interested and asked the sergeant if he could arrange for him to join; the old sergeant smiled and said, "I think I can do that for you, son."

In just a short while, the old sergeant approached and told John that everything was worked out so he could join the army, and before John knew what was happening, he was holding up his right hand and taking the oath to protect the United States from all enemies, foreign and domestic.

After being sworn into the army, John was ordered to San Francisco, where he was held for several weeks, waiting for enough recruits to make a full load for the voyage to the Philippines. In a few weeks, a sufficient number of recruits had arrived, so they boarded the *USS Republic* and set sail for the Philippines. On the way west, they stopped for several days at Pearl Harbor, picking up a few more recruits. John enjoyed his time at Pearl Harbor, having never seen an environment like the one there.

Upon arriving in Manila, John was assigned to the Thirty-First Infantry Regiment at Fort McKinley. The Thirty-First had never been stationed in the United States and had always been an overseas unit. As it would turn out, many of the soldiers who were forced to endure the infamous Bataan Death March took their training with him at Fort McKinley.

While there, the recruits received training in close-order drill, marching, calisthenics, street fighting with bayonets, shooting, and hand-to-hand combat. An integral part of basic training was camouflage techniques. John felt he had been wrongly kicked out of the CCC and took the opportunity to excel in all aspects of training, especially in camouflage techniques. He did, in fact, do extremely well and received several commendations for his excellent performance as a recruit.

One of his instructors for basic training, Corporal Motolla, was especially helpful to all the recruits during this time. He took a special interest in John's training since John seemed to be working so hard not only to do well, but to excel in all aspects of basic training. John remembered that Motolla especially stressed that when the recruits were crawling on the ground, they should keep their behinds down to keep from getting shot there. John said that Corporal Motolla emphasized this to him forcefully because he had a tendency to crawl with his rear end high.

"Corporal Motolla," John said, "taught us skills while we were in basic training that became second nature to us as we fought the Japanese. His training saved many of our lives"

Four

While they were taking their basic training, the reins were held pretty tightly on the recruits. But when the training ended, things began to improve for John and the others. They were given time off after their normal daily activities, so the soldiers would go into town and mingle with the local citizens. They would go to movies, walk on the beach, visit museums, and otherwise learn about the city.

Like most of the new soldiers, John was too young to go into bars, which were in great abundance. He had learned to dance while in Oregon, where he had attended dances with other soldiers and local young people. There were skating rinks in several locations, so he decided that he would like to learn to skate.

So John sought out one of the more popular skating rinks, rented shoes, and began to try to skate. He soon noticed a very attractive young girl who was having trouble standing up on her skates. He approached her and asked if he could help, to which she replied that she would welcome some help.

John helped her stand, and they skated slowly around the rink. They were both beginners, so they had to be very careful to avoid falling. Of this meeting, John said, "I felt like this was the love of my life almost from the moment I met her. She was young, pretty, and had a hauntingly beautiful sense about her that attracted me strongly." But he quickly learned that he and Juanita could not be alone at any time; her family's culture required that a chaperone had to be with them at all times.

As they got to know each other, John learned that she was one of eight children, all girls. She had a twin sister who had died in infancy. Juanita was very shy and reserved, and it was a long time before she could work up the courage to tell John how she felt about him. At this time, Juanita was 27 years old.

He learned that her father was a US soldier stationed in the Philippines who had been diagnosed with diabetes. Soon after his diagnosis, he had been ordered back to the United States to be treated and had died in a hospital in the States.

He further learned that Juanita's parents were not married. When her father had been ordered back to the States for treatment, all the girls had been placed in foster homes. They were treated so badly that all of the girls ran away and soon became wards of the state. As wards, they were sent to a convent where they were required to stay until they were twenty-one years of age.

As a young girl, Juanita had been very quiet and reserved, talked very little, and always stayed in the background. As a result of her introverted behavior, her sisters concluded that she was mentally challenged. When the girls were sent to the convent, her sisters told the nuns in the convent that she was a slow learner.

Upon being told this about Juanita, the nuns saw this as a challenge and began working closely with Juanita in all her studies. With all the special attention she received, the nuns were pleasantly surprised to learn that Juanita not a dullard and that she was quite bright, talented, and could learn and retain her lessons very effectively. With the encouragement and help of the nuns, Juanita not only blossomed as a student, but she began to tutor other students as well. While still in high school, Juanita enrolled in a commercial school and excelled to the point that she graduated from that school before she graduated from high school.

As the weeks and months passed, John and Juanita spent all their spare time together, with the the chaperone, an older sister, always present. John's love for Juanita increased, and they spent many happy moments together as they walked on the beach, strolled through parks, and enjoyed every meeting to the fullest. He visited her at her home on many occasions and was welcomed by her family members, who were always glad to see him. He would often save fruit from the mess hall and carry it to the family when he visited Juanita.

Five

The Imperial Japanese Navy carried out a surprise attack on Pearl Harbor the morning of December 7, 1941. The strike led the United States into World War II.[2] Ten hours later, on December 8, the Japanese began their invasion of the Philippines.[3]

On the day of the attack, John and Juanita attended a party for employees of the company where she worked. Her boss was hosting the party as an early Christmas party for the employees to show his appreciation for all their hard work during the year.

---

2 "Attack on Pearl Harbor," n64, *Wikipedia*, http://en.wikipedia.org/. (Accessed 11-23-15)

3 Ibid.

Suddenly they began to hear planes flying nearby and bombs exploding. At first, they thought the Japanese were bombing Manila, but Manila was spared.

Upon hearing the planes and bombs, John took Juanita to the safety of her home. He then returned to his base, ran to the arms storeroom, and took a Browning Automatic Rifle (BAR), a Thompson sub-machine gun, a rifle, and all the ammunition he could carry. He ran to a pillbox, situated himself, and began firing the BAR at the planes. When he had used all the ammunition for the BAR, he threw it down, picked up the Thompson submachine gun, and fired it until he had exhausted its ammunition. He then picked up his Springfield rifle and fired it, reloading as soon as the last bullet in the clip was gone. Soldiers were everywhere it seemed, firing rifles, machine guns, and BARs at the planes as they released bombs, strafed, and generally wreaked havoc.

John said, "The Japanese were flying so low and so slowly that I could see the faces of the pilots as they flew by while I was shooting at them; they were smiling at me as they dropped their bombs and strafed us. Some of them even waved at us as they flew by."

When the bombing and strafing ended, the troops regrouped and went to their assigned duty stations.

John was assigned to a .50-caliber machine gun as he and his comrades prepared for the anticipated Japanese invasion. When it came, they were attacked by well-trained and well-armed troops. Fighting was fierce for days as the Japanese slowly advanced, driving the American and Filipino troops farther inland.

At the time of the attack, John was stationed in Manila at Cartel de España, in the Walled City (which is the oldest district and historic core of Manila). Fighting continued sporadically until December 26, 1941, when the defending troops left. Manila was declared an open city (that is, the government declared it had abandoned all defensive efforts) to save it from complete destruction.

At that time, most of the troops were ordered to Bataan, where the resistance continued to be fierce. John and his unit were ordered to Corregidor, where they fought for about a week. Bataan is a small peninsula on the west coast, south of Manila, and Corregidor is a small island off Bataan.

Before leaving Manila, John left the personal items that he could not take to Corregidor with Juanita and her family, hoping that they would be able to use or sell them to buy food for themselves. John learned later that Juanita had been successful in selling some of his belongings. On Corregidor, fighting became ferocious. While there John said that the American and Filipino soldiers had the advantage. They killed many more Japanese than the number of Americans and Filipinos killed. On the island, eroded, dead volcanoes formed circular "bowls," usually open at one end and heavy with vegetation. This particular topographical characteristic gave great advantage to the American and Filipino soldiers, who would hide in the jungle vegetation where they could see the Japanese but could not be seen. They hid and waited for the advancing Japanese soldiers, who had to enter the "bowl" through a low spot on one side. They waited until the Japanese were forced closer together by the natural terrain. When the order to fire was shouted, shots rained down on the Japanese from three sides of the "bowl" in a great fusillade of fire. John said, "The Japanese were forced to move closer to each other as they entered the field of fire. When we began to shoot at them, it was almost impossible not to hit one of them because they were so close together." Few defenders were killed, but the Japanese deaths mounted into the hundreds.

The battle on Corregidor continued for about a week, after which John and his unit were ordered to re-form on Bataan. When they received the order to move, they loaded as many of their supplies as possible onto trucks for transport to their new location. Supplies that could not be moved were taken to a nearby arena, piled high, and burned. Barracks and headquarters buildings, vehicles and machinery that could not be taken, and gasoline storage tanks and bridges were blown up and destroyed.

John said, "One of the wonders of that period was that the doctors on Corregidor and Bataan did such a marvelous job of caring for the wounded, from the mildest of wounds to life-threatening injuries. Many of those soldiers lived to fight again because of the excellent medical treatment they received under almost impossible conditions."

When the Japanese captured Manila, civilians, especially American, were captured and placed in detention centers. Juanita was among those captured. She was thought to be American, so she was placed in a small cage and put on display in the square. Her mother went to the Japanese commander and asked why he had done this. The commander yelled, "She American!" Her mother told the commander that Juanita was not American, but was Spanish. As a result, Juanita was released from the cage and allowed to reunite with the rest of her family.

When the Japanese learned of Juanita's educational background, she was drafted to work in the Japanese commander's office. She had a shortwave radio hidden in the office. When questioned by the Japanese as to the radio's whereabouts, she stated that someone had stolen it during all the confusion of the invasion. Juanita was able to gather intelligence about the Japanese forces since she worked in their headquarters. Based on messages she had secretly received from John and at great risk to her life, she occasionally used the radio to send intelligence on the status of the prisoners to General MacArthur's headquarters

John had earlier warned her not to share any information about anything to anyone, saying that anything she shared with others might be passed on to the Japanese as a way to gain favor. This counsel from John proved to be wise advice since many of her acquaintances, including all of her sisters, were killed by the Japanese for what they considered espionage.

Six

Earlier in 1941, General Douglas MacArthur had been recalled to active duty as commander of US Army Forces in the Far East.[4] In August, he requested 84,500 Garand rifles, 330 .30-caliber machine guns, 326 .50-caliber machine guns, 450 37-mm guns, 217 81-mm mortars, 288 75-mm guns, and more than 8,000 vehicles. On September 8, he was informed that he would not receive most of these items. As a result, the troops were forced to continue using older, bolt-action Enfield and Springfield rifles.[5]

---

4 "Douglas MacArthur in World War II," *Wikipedia*, http://en.wikipedia.org/. (Accessed 11-23-15)
5 "Military History of the Philippines during World War II," *Wikipedia*, http://en.wikipedia.org (Accessed 11-23-15)

So when the Japanese attacked the Philippines, the defenders had obsolete arms, but the army still fought brilliantly against the invaders.

John said, "We knew the lay of the land and could take advantage of that knowledge to ambush the Japs when and where they least expected it. As time passed, and our supply of ammunition began to give out, we had to ambush the Japs when we came across small patrols or a group of just two or three enemy soldiers."

Of the Japanese battle plan, John said, "The Japs thought they could overtake the Philippines in two or three weeks, but it didn't happen that way. The first general to bring his troops onto the island was soundly defeated. Soon thereafter a second general brought his troops into the fight, and they too were defeated. We held out until April 9, 1942, when we were finally ordered to surrender."

During those four months while the Americans and Filipinos were fighting the Japanese, John found that he used many of the skills he had learned as a young boy and in basic training. Walking stealthily as his uncles had taught him, he was able to infiltrate enemy lines time after time. The primary purpose of those excursions was to gather intelligence: How many Japanese were there, how close were they, and what was likely to be their next move?

The information that John collected in this manner was invaluable to American troops. Many times the intelligence that John gathered allowed them to position themselves so they could more successfully ambush the advancing enemy.

John described the manner in which he entered enemy-held territory: "I was very careful about how I moved into their territory. I was able to walk silently into and through the places where they were holed up. Many times I was seen by one or more of the Japanese; when they saw me, they would simply nod at me or raise a hand. I simply replied with a wave or nod of my head and kept on going about my business. Being Native American, I suppose I looked enough like one of them that they never challenged me."

On many of these excursions into the camps, John was able to help himself to Japanese food. He often returned with bags of rice, canned fruit, canned oysters, sugar, and others supplies useful to himself and his comrades.

During the four months of fighting, the number of able-bodied defenders gradually reduced. As a result, they had to rely on guerilla tactics against the Japanese.

They attacked the enemy using whatever weapons they had available.

One technique used in these guerilla operations was described by John as follows: "We would try to find a lone soldier, or two, and silently work our way behind them. When we were in position, one of us would get the attention of the enemy. While the Jap focused his attention on the lone American, we would quietly sneak up behind the Jap soldier, grab him, and shove a bayonet in him or hold him by the head as we cut his throat, holding his mouth shut so he could not call out to his comrades."

Once the Japanese soldier was dead, the GIs would take his gun, ammunition, and the pack in which he carried water and food. They also took any clothing that they might be able to use.

This technique worked well. If the Americans happened to come upon a place where the Japanese had put down their packs, perhaps to swim or bathe in a nearby stream, they would take anything they could use and disappear into the surrounding jungle.

When the Japanese troops moved onto the Bataan peninsula, the Americans were bombarded with cannons and air attacks. The defenders of Bataan fought bravely for weeks. Attacks by the Japanese from various quarters were met with fierce resistance. John summed up these numerous attacks: "We lost a lot of men, but the Japanese lost many times more men than we did. We fought as if our lives depended on it because they did."

But as fiercely and as bravely as they fought, the defending forces were quickly running out of food, ammunition, and medicine. The Americans were not receiving any supplies from America, whereas the Japanese troops were receiving both personnel reinforcements and supplies on a regular basis.

The fighting was intense on all fronts. The defenders fought with continually dwindling amounts of troops and ammunition. After about five weeks, commanders of the various units received a letter dated January 15, 1942, from General MacArthur's headquarters with orders that the letter be read to all troops in all commands. The letter read in part:

"Help is on the way from the U.S. Thousands of troops and hundreds of planes are being dispatched. The exact time of arrival is unknown. (sic) as they will have to fight their way through the Japs against them. It is imperative that our troops hold until the reinforcements arrive(sic) no further retreat is possible. We have more troops in Bataan than the Japs have thrown against us, our supplies are ample; a determined defense will defeat the enemy's attack."[6]

Soon after the letter from MacArthur was read to the soldiers, "MacArthur was ordered by President Roosevelt to relocate to Australia. MacArthur discussed the idea with his staff that he resign his commission and fight as a private soldier in the Philippine resistance, but Sutherland [Lt. Col. Richard K. Sutherland, one of MacArthur's staff] talked him out of it. On the night of March 12, 1942, MacArthur and a select group…left Corregidor in four PT boats… MacArthur and his party reached Del Monte Airfield in Bukidnon province on the island of Mindanao two days later. General George Marshall sent three US Navy B-17s to pick them up. Two of them arrived and brought the entire group to Australia."[7]

With this promise of aid from MacArthur, the troops fought valiantly and long. They waited through January, through February, through March, and into early April. While they fought and waited for the promised relief, innumerable soldiers performed above and

---

6 From letter dated January 15, 1942, from MacArthur's headquarters.

7 "Douglas MacArthur in World War II, Philippines Campaign (1941–42) Escape to Australia and Medal of Honor Citation," *Wikipedia*, http:// en.wikipedia.org/. (Accessed 11-23-15)

beyond their duty and what could be expected of any foot soldier. There was no time or desire to document the heroics of the average soldier. Each one did what he could do and more than was expected. Each was majestically heroic, and no man sought medals or recognition for that superior performance on the field of battle. They simply did what soldiers do: their jobs.

No replacements were forthcoming. In the meantime, the Japanese were receiving regular replacements of food, ammunition, and troops. While the number of defenders was slowly being reduced, the invaders constantly added to their numbers.

Seven

The Surrender and the March

After MacArthur left for Australia, General Jonathan M. Wainwright IV was appointed to succeed MacArthur as general of the armies of the Philippines while King General Edward P. King became commanding general of the Philippine-American forces on the Bataan peninsula.[8]

Then, after months of fighting and with food and medicine exhausted, King surrendered his troops on April 9, 1942. Wainwright and his 10,000 men held on

---

8 "Edward P. King—World War II," *Wikipedia*, http://en.wikipedia.org/. (Accessed 11-22-15)

to Corregidor until on May 6, they too were forced to surrender.[9]

After the order to surrender was issued, many of the soldiers, American and Filipino, did so. Some refused to surrender and took to the jungle with their weapons to hide out and harass the Japanese for the duration of the war. Some of the troops held out for weeks before surrendering. Of the order to surrender, John said, "When we were ordered to surrender, we were told where to stack our rifles. My unit refused to stack our rifles where ordered; instead we laid them down in creeks where we could recover them to continue fighting when we got supplies and if we could escape."

John reported that when they surrendered, the Japanese made them remove all of their clothing, including their shoes and hats, permitting them to wear only shorts or a G-string around their groin area. All their valuables were taken from them by the Japanese soldiers.

It is estimated that seventy-five-thousand soldiers were taken prisoner after the surrender of Bataan—twelve-thousand Americans and sixty-three-thousand

---

9 Ibid.

Filipinos.[10] John said that they were ordered to line up four abreast and begin to march. John's foursome in the march consisted of himself, a captain (name forgotten), John Freeman, and James Snyder from Charlotte, North Carolina.

As the prisoners began to march, a soda dropped from a bag on a sergeant's Harley-Davidson motorcycle. As it fell, the soda rolled near John's feet. Seeing this John stepped over, picked up the soda, handed it to the sergeant, and got back in line. Some of the other guards witnessed what had happened and immediately began yelling at the sergeant, who then called out to John.

Hearing the words of his fellow soldiers, the sergeant hit John in the face with the soda, a glass bottle, knocking out several teeth and breaking John's jaw. John fell to the ground and nearly died from the blood and loose teeth in his mouth.

After John fell, the other men in his group quickly picked him up, and they began marching again. After John had been picked up, the sergeant told John, "I had to do that; if I had not, I would have lost too much face."

---

10 "About Education, The Bataan Death March, The Man Held Responsible," *Wikipedia*, http://en.wikipedia.org/. (Accessed 11-23-15)

They marched, holding John up, and after only a hundred yards or so, John told his companions, "Fellows, I just blacked out." When he awakened, one of his companions gave him a drink of water from his canteen. John said the water was thick and tasted like mud.

As they marched, they learned that the Japanese guard who had hit John in the face with the soda bottle had been educated in America. He had been a policeman in Tokyo and had not wanted to be in the army. John and his companions asked where they were being taken. The sergeant replied, "We don't have a place for you. You are supposed to die on this march."

John related how soldiers who were unable to march were killed by the Japanese. Some of the wounded began the march but eventually became so weak they could not go any further. When a soldier fell, one of the Japanese would immediately kill him, sometimes with a bullet but usually with his bayonet. The bullets were saved for later use. Some of the Japanese officers who rode horses would use their swords to severe the heads from those who fell. John remarked, "I saw all of these things and more. We were in constant danger of losing our lives."

Many of the weakened soldiers were held up by others in their foursome as they marched. In many cases, their companions finally became too weak to help further, so they fell and were immediately executed.

About 2,500 to 10,000 Filipino and 100 to 650 US prisoners of war died before they reached their destination.[11] John noted that the Japanese gave the prisoners little food and water and that some of the guards cruelly allowed the prisoners no food or water. He said that as they marched, when they crossed a creek, anyone seen by those guards taking a drink was immediately bayoneted. John further noted that some of the guards were more humane than others and would turn their heads when they came upon a source of water, allowing the prisoners to drink.

On several occasions, upon seeing water, John told the men it was unsafe to drink because there were dead bodies lying in the water, both humans and animals. Some were so thirsty that they drank the water anyhow and ended up dying horrible deaths as fever overtook them. After this occurred several times, the prisoners began to rely on John to approve of any water they drank.

The severity of the prisoners' ill treatment was unexpected and overwhelming. John thought there

---

11 "Bataan Death March [5][6][7]," *Wikipedia*, http://en.wikipedia.org/. (Accessed 11-23-15)

were two possible reasons for such inhumane treatment of the prisoners:

1. The Japanese were so cruel to the prisoners in retribution for the fierce resistance that the American and Filipino soldiers had put up in killing thousands of their soldiers.
2. They were so cruel because they were treated so harshly by their officers. It was not uncommon for a Japanese officer to hit a Japanese soldier in the face with his hand for any minor show of disrespect.

As they marched, Filipino citizens hiding in the surrounding bushes would toss rice cakes and sugar cakes to the prisoners. John said, "Any prisoner who was seen to catch and eat the rice cakes or sugar cakes was killed immediately." He continued, "Whenever the Japs caught one of the Filipinos who had tossed the food to the prisoners, that person was tortured until he or she died. We were forced to form a circle around the person as the Japs tortured the person until the person died. What they did to those people was ungodly. That was one reason why we loved the Filipinos so much. They would do anything they could to try to help us, even at the loss of their own lives."

Having learned so much about the forest and its plants as a youngster in Florida, John was able to use that knowledge to help him identify plants that were edible, providing nutrition for himself and others on the death march. For example, while in basic training, John had learned about a lettuce-looking plant that grew plentifully in the forest where there was a small amount of moisture in the soil.

During the march, John spotted some of the plants. When guards were not watching closely, he would grab some of the plant, eating some and then sharing with others, being careful not to get caught. The plant had a pleasing taste and provided some nutrition to the prisoners. John felt that his knowledge of this particular plant was instrumental in saving many prisoners' lives.

During the march, the prisoners had to sleep outdoors, lying wherever they could find a place. One night they came to a schoolhouse with a fenced-in playground. The prisoners were packed into the area so tightly that no one could lie down. They had to spend the night standing up, sleeping as best as they could.

The marching continued for about a month, first in one direction and then back the way they had come. Thousands died in that month. Hunger was a constant companion of the prisoners. Just about all of them suffered from beriberi, dysentery, anemia, malaria, and other debilitating maladies. The doctors did what they could for the prisoners, having no medicine to treat them.

Ever-present hunger was a problem for the prisoners and never took a day off. They had to scrounge for everything they ate. One kind of relief came from the Japanese themselves. The guards ate a lot of fish with their rice and other meager food supplies.

When the guards cleaned their fish, the prisoners begged them for the heads, which the guards sometimes tossed to them and sometimes threw into the garbage, where they were retrieved. The fish heads were used to make a stew or soup that the prisoners often ate along with seaweed or some leafy plants. The plants lost volume after being cooked but helped fill their bellies. John credited the fish stew and the cooked plants with saving the lives of many prisoners.

Eight

LIFE AS A PRISONER

The prisoners eventually arrived at Camp O'Donnell where they were finally allowed to stop marching. Rice paddies continued to be their living quarters at night. There were no barracks for the prisoners. They had to spend their nights lying in the mud and water. There was no cover to keep rain and insects off them. They were subjected to constant attack by insects that seemed determined to suck the life out of each prisoner. All during the night, the pests flew, bit, and sucked a little more life from the frail and depleted body of each prisoner.

They were forced to work during the day to grow vegetables for their own consumption. Until their crops produced food, they had to do the best they could to feed themselves. The knowledge some of the prisoners had about edible plants gave them some sustenance but not the protein and fat their bodies needed. Besides the fish stew they were able to make, the prisoners had little food.

After a couple of weeks, the prisoners were moved from Camp O'Donnell to Camp Cabanatuan, where there were barracks in which the prisoners could sleep. There they were sheltered from both the frequent rain and the furious insect attacks. It was not complete relief, but it was a pleasant change.

John considered both O'Donnell and Cabanatuan to be "the worst places under the sun." Conditions in both prisons were deplorable, but at least the prisoners had a roof over their heads at Camp Cabanatuan.

Death was a daily occurrence as men died from starvation, disease, or injuries received from numerous beatings. Some simply gave up, broken in spirit and body. One of those who just gave up was the captain who was in the foursome with John when the march began.

Another cause of death for many prisoners was contamination of the food grown in the rice paddies. The Japanese soldiers used human excrement to fertilize their crops. The odor in those areas was terrible. Aware of the possible health problems, most of the prisoners avoided eating any food grown in the rice paddies.

Some of the prisoners were so hungry that they ate the food anyway, becoming infected to the point that their limbs swelled up to three or four times their normal size and eventually bursting! The lack of medicine with which to treat these prisoners resulted in most of them dying horribly painful deaths.

Dozens of soldiers died each day at both Camp O'Donnell and Camp Cabanatuan. John was among those who daily carried the dead bodies of his fellow soldiers to mass graves outside the camps. The Japanese, using captured American bulldozers, dug long trenches to hold the dead. The bodies were carried out by work details and thrown into the trenches. This activity took place several times a day. The bodies were then covered over with dirt pushed into the graves by the bulldozers.

Some of the soldiers who were thrown into the graves were still alive. From time to time, one of the soldiers would awaken and try to crawl out. Upon seeing this, a Japanese soldier would simply walk over to the revived soldier and shove his bayonet into him.

In spite of all this depravity by the guards, the living had to focus on just that: living. They had to harness all their remaining, though dwindling, strength to surviving for another day, which was a constant challenge. They had to fight hunger, thirst, and an assortment of diseases.

While John was at Camp Cabanatuan, he would occasionally see Juanita outside the barbed-wire fence surrounding the compound. That was her way of letting him know that she was waiting for his return. At times they were able to send and receive messages from each other. Surprisingly some of the guards were willing to carry messages between the prisoners and their loved ones. This enabled John to pass on information about the treatment of the prisoners, which Juanita was able to send to MacArthur's headquarters using the shortwave radio hidden in the office where she worked.

The fight to survive included bouts of malnutrition stemming from the very meager rations, dysentery, malaria, and a host of other debilitating diseases and circumstances. John suffered from several of those maladies. At one point he was so sick and weak that he was put into a clinic to be looked after by the doctors.

These clinics were named Ward Zero through Ward Four. The least serious illnesses were place in Ward Four. As the illness progressed, prisoners were move to Ward Three, then Ward Two, and then Ward One. The most seriously ill prisoners who were not expected to live were placed in Ward Zero. John said, "I was placed in Ward Zero several times, but each night I crawled back to Ward Four." On one of those returns to Ward Four, John passed out just outside the ward and was found the next morning, lying on the ground. "A naval doctor," John said, "fed me some scorched rice. That stopped my dysentery and helped me keep food on my stomach, and that is what saved me."

After John recovered from this bout of illness, the doctor was able to have him transferred to Clark Field, where he was one of several prisoners assigned the responsibility of keeping the grass cut on the airfield and surrounding area. There were several prisoners there who were interested in learning to speak Japanese and Chinese, and some wanted to learn Spanish.

John had begun to learn Spanish soon after he arrived in the Philippines. There were others who spoke Japanese. John taught those who wanted to learn Spanish, and another prisoner taught those who wanted to learn Japanese. John was an adept student and learned Japanese more quickly than the others.

John soon developed fluency in Japanese, which the Japanese guards and officers noticed. As a result of his learning the language so well, he noticed that the guards seemed to show a modicum of respect he had not known before. He was soon assigned duty as a runner, carrying messages between several of the Japanese camps.

After a period of time as a runner, John became familiar to the guards at the various camps, and he was watched less closely than he had been before. As a result, he was able to steal medicine and food to carry back to his camp on several occasions. It was always a gamble for him to take these items, but he considered it worth a beating should he get caught.

The prisoners hatched a scheme involving a C-47 transport airplane at Clark Field that had been pushed off to the side of the runway and never flown again. They planned to get the plane airworthy so they could steal it and fly it to a US-controlled area.

Among the prisoners were mechanics and pilots, so there was plenty of knowledge of what had to be done to get the plane in flying condition. They worked for several weeks and finally had it ready to fly.

On the night they had planned to escape, the prisoners got to the airfield only to discover that the plane had been moved. They never knew who told the Japanese of their plans, but they figured that a fellow prisoner, in order to gain favor and privileges from the guards, told them about the plan.

Nine

ESCAPE AND CAPTURE

Security at Clark Field was such that on occasion, prisoners would sneak out of the encampment at night in search of food. John himself had done this several times. One night he was caught and brought back for punishment. Fortunately he was not slain immediately upon capture.

The guards brought John back, and he was laid down in front of a bulldozer. The blade was put down on his legs, crushing them. He was then placed in a dungeon where he received little medical care. John does not know who brought him food, but he said that every time he saw that it had been placed in his cell, "I ate it like a dog."

The Filipinos knew John was in the dungeon, and sometimes some of the women would throw rice cakes through the narrow window for him. He was very grateful for the food, saying that it probably kept him from starving to death while he was there. Knowing how the Japanese were, John knew that had a guard seen the Filipinos throwing the rice cakes to him, they would have been killed. After his legs healed, he was taken back to be with the other prisoners.

John, as well as other prisoners, frequently endured harsh beatings. The guards could manufacture an excuse at any time to beat any prisoner. John said, "Several times after having been tortured and beaten, I was asked by the guard doing the beating, 'Why don't you die, American?' I simply responded, 'Because God loves me.'"

John added, "Each time I gave that response to a guard, he would have a troubled look on his face as if he knew exactly what I was talking about."

After he recovered from the crushing of his legs by the bulldozer blade, John was moved to Camp Bilibid. John considered Bilibid prison to be even worse than the prisons at Camp O'Donnell and Camp Cabanatuan. While conditions in those camps were horrible, at Bilibid, his cell was incredibly filthy, with human excrement and urine on the floor. John said, "I was scared to death while I was there because there were rats as big as cats running in and out of my cell all the time. I was afraid of having rats eat me in my sleep."

Ten

SLAVE LABOR IN JAPAN

The Japanese needed labor in the coal mines in Japan. On several occasions, prisoners from islands held by the Japanese were placed on ships and taken to work in the mines. After he had been at Bilibid for a short time, John was placed on a broken-down steamer with several thousand other prisoners. They made stops in several ports in Vietnam, Korea, and China along the way. It took the ship sixty-two days to complete the voyage.

During the trip, prisoners were placed in the crowded holds below deck, with no portholes and little ventilation. The hold was adjacent to the engine room, and it was very hot the entire voyage.

John said that the prisoners intended to over-whelm the crew and take over the ship, but each time they were ready to put their plan into action, the ship broke down. Not knowing how to repair the ship, they would abandon their plan. They had hoped, just as with the airplane, to sail it to an area controlled by Americans.

When the ship finally arrived in Japan, the vast majority of the prisoners had died. Only a very small percentage of those put on board were still alive. The hot temperature, lack of food and water, and lingering illnesses killed most of them.

In "Death on the Hellships at Sea in the Pacific War," Gregory Michno estimated that more than 126,000 Allied prisoners of war were transported on 156 voyages on 134 Japanese merchant ships. More than 21,000 Americans were killed or injured from "friendly fire" by US submarines or planes as a result of being prisoners on what survivors called "hell ships."[12]

John said that prisoners who worked all day in the mines were given a rice cake; those who did not work received about half a rice cake. The labor was tedious

---

12 Lee A. Gladwin, "American POWs on Japanese Ships Take a Voyage into Hell," *Prologue Magazine* 35, no. 4 (Winter 2003).

and demanding, and the prisoners were constantly harassed and forced to work hard. Beatings of those whom the Japanese did not think were working hard enough were commonplace.

One day as a detail of one hundred prisoners was returning from the mines, one of the prisoners sneaked out of formation, went into a nearby garden, stole some onions, and got back into formation with the others. One of the Japanese guards saw this but said nothing at the time.

When the prisoners arrived back at their barracks, the guards told the prisoners that they had seen one of them sneak out of formation, enter a garden, and steal some food. The prisoners were told that unless the guilty party stepped forward, all one hundred of the prisoners would be beaten severely.

The prisoner who had stolen the onions was a diminutive man who began to shake uncontrollably when he heard what the guards planned. On seeing the terror in the small man, John said, "I don't know what came over me, but I stepped forward, and the rest of the group was allowed to go into the barracks. I knew the Lord was with me."

After the other prisoners were in the barracks, John received a beating that was simply inhumane. He was hit repeatedly with the butts of rifles and sticks, kicked all over his body, and stepped on. Of the beating, John said, "While they were beating me, I felt every blow. And suddenly my spirit was above where I was lying as they beat me. I could see them beating me, but I could not feel anything. While I was in the air looking down at the scene, I saw angels and a valley. I saw the other side; everything was nice. It was beautiful."

When the beating stopped and John's spirit reentered his body, the guards dragged him over to the barracks, where they put a noose around his neck. They pulled it tight and hanged him so that his toes could barely touch the ground. They left him hanging for several hours. When they let him down, besides a broken arm, leg, and ribs, he had ugly bruises over his entire body and three broken vertebrae in his neck.

When asked why he thought he was so frequently the target of beatings, John replied, "I think the primary reason they picked on me and beat me so much was because I had blond hair and blue eyes, and they just wanted to eliminate those colors."

Eleven

John endured and survived another of his many beatings, this one in Japan not long before the war ended. A guard was talking to John, who responded in Japanese, "Is that so?" The guard told John that he had answered in a disrespectful manner and that was the cause for the beating.

Not long after that beating, on August 15, 1945, John was in the barracks one evening at about dusk and heard a Japanese sergeant talking to some of the guards just outside. Having a knowledge of Japanese, John understood every word the sergeant said, with the exception of one word.

John asked a major at the camp to get a Japanese dictionary so he could look up the meaning of that word. When John got the dictionary, he looked up the word, which turned out to be "unconditional." Upon learning this, he told the major and others nearby that the war had been over since the day before, August 14, when the Japanese had surrendered unconditionally.

Having learned that the war was over, John said that he immediately looked up at the guard who had so recently given him the severe beating because, in the guard's words, he had answered him in a "disrespectful" manner. When he found the guard, he greeted the man in a friendly manner and told him that the war was over. The guard asked John how he knew that. John smiled at him and said, "A little bird flew into the compound and told me and then flew back out."

John said, "When I told him that, he dropped his rifle and ran away from the compound as fast as he could, and I never saw him again." By way of explaining the guard's quick departure, John said, "My belief is that he thought the prisoners would retaliate for all the harsh treatment they had received at the hand of the guards, and this one in particular."

The next morning, there were no Japanese in the compound. The prisoners were free to come and go as they wished, but many were reluctant to leave. John was one of many who did leave to go into the nearby village to find food. But they found that the local people were very poor and had little to eat themselves. The people were friendly and kind to the prisoners, but they had no food to share because they were poor.

It was two long months before a train could be scheduled to go into the village where the prisoners were held. Damage to trains and rail lines contributed to the delay.

After a short period of time, American planes found the compound. Soon more planes appeared and dropped food, clothing, and medicine. The prisoners were elated to have such an abundance. John said that the food was shared with the people in the village, who thanked them profusely.

From the time the war ended until they were able to leave the area, there were no abuses of the local Japanese people by the former prisoners. Even though the prisoners had been harshly treated by the Japanese guards, the prisoners did not take it out on the local people.

American rescue parties were sent out across Japan to prisoner-of-war camps to gather up surviving prisoners to be brought back to hospital ships. There they were given medical exams, treated for their maladies, fed, allowed to bathe, and given new clothing. John said they were told that Eleanor Roosevelt, President Roosevelt's wife, had said that she did not want the soldiers returned to America in their emaciated condition. She wanted "some flesh" put on their bones before returning to the United States.

Not long after being taken aboard a hospital ship, John and the others made the return trip to the Philippines. John had been put aboard the ship to be sent from the Philippines to Japan in October 1944. It had been almost a year since he had been shipped from Camp Bilibid to Japan.

Shortly after arriving back in the Philippines, John saw one of the men who had been in his foursome during the death march, John Freeman. They had not seen each other since John had been transferred to Clark Field, which had been well over a year before.

John learned that Freeman had been back in the Philippines for about a month and that he had just returned from seeing Juanita. Freeman told John that as soon as he returned to the Philippines, he had looked for Juanita, found her, and tried to court her, but she would have none of it. She told Freeman quickly and firmly that she was waiting only for John Mims.

Freeman was about to get on a ship to return to the United States when the two met. Mims told Freeman that he was not going anywhere until he took Mims to see Juanita. They soon arrived where Juanita was working as a waitress. Upon seeing him, she rushed into John's arms. They embraced each other strongly as they kissed and tears fell. The reunion was everything John had hoped it would be.

John returned to the replacement depot where he had been assigned and immediately filed paperwork for permission to be married. He said that it took only two or three days for approval, and they were married within the week.

John & Juanita Mims Wedding photo

Twelve

Two or three months later, John was ordered back to the United States, where he took prisoner's survival leave. He was sent to the Cromwell Hotel in Miami Beach. John rested and relaxed as he slowly learned to enjoy the beach atmosphere. John was in Miami at the Cromwell Hotel for about ninety days, during which time all his expenses were paid by the army.

While he was in Oregon, he had learned to dance and thought himself to be a fairly good dancer. He felt so confident in his skills that he answered an ad seeking someone to teach young ladies to dance. John said that the girls had come from up north for the winter with their parents and were encouraged to learn to dance. John taught dancing for about five weeks, working two or three hours a day and two or three days a week.

After his survivor's leave, he was ordered to Fort McPherson near Atlanta, where Juanita soon joined him. While there, he was assigned to the supply depot. His duties included overseeing the filling of supply orders from various bases in several states. He was diligent in seeing that all requests for supplies left McPherson in a timely manner. In addition to those duties, he taught ROTC classes at Boys' High School and at Tech High School for two years.

He served several years in Japan where he was in charge of the quartermaster depot as master sergeant. As he had in Fort McPherson, he was responsible for ensuring that orders for supplies from bases in the Far East were filled completely and in a timely manner. The depot, under John's management, was very efficient in getting all orders for supplies shipped without delay.

Besides serving at Fort McPherson, John also served in the same quartermaster role at Fort Jackson in South Carolina and Fort Bragg in North Carolina.

While he was at Fort Bragg, the army began developing an interest in special forces. President

John F. Kennedy learned of this program and became very intrigued by the concept. He visited Fort Bragg, and in seeking personnel with knowledge of and experience in guerilla fighting, John Mims's name was among several which came up.

The president talked with John and others about their backgrounds in guerilla fighting. As a result of these conversations, John and others spent hours talking with special forces personnel, sharing in detail what they knew on the subject. The special-forces troops picked their brains as they sought all the information they could to further their knowledge of that tactic.

John told of his experiences in his excursions into the Japanese-controlled areas, telling them about his stealthy movements and his knowledge of camouflage techniques. All the hours interviewing John and the others resulted in knowledge the army used to develop its training program and operations plans. A large part of the techniques and battle plans in US Army Special Forces have the imprint of John Mims.

Thirteen

REDEMPTION

In October 2012 John was favored with a chance to visit Japan through the Japanese/American POW Friendship Program. This trip included a visit to the coal mine where he worked as slave labor near the prison camp, Mini City. This was where he had been so severely beaten and hung, coming close to death.

Citizens in the village near the camp came out to recognize and honor the former prisoners. John and other former prisoners were given the chance to share their experiences with the audience. John told them about the suffering he had undergone, having been beaten and hung and so close to death while at Mini City.

He also told them that he had, by the grace of God, forgiven the Japanese guards who treated the prisoners so harshly, but that he had not forgotten.

A memorial park had been built near the coal mine. One of the coordinators for the park development was a man whom John had met after the Japanese surrendered. It was a memorable meeting as they shared recollections of the beating to which John had referred. The man had been a young boy and saw the beating and saw John being hung. He told John his mother had desperately tried to get him away from witnessing the beating and hanging. She had not wanted her son to watch the brutality being shown by the guards as they beat John relentlessly.

Epilogue

Master Sergeant John Mims retired from the army in 1964 after having served honorably for more than twenty-three years. During their marriage, John and Juanita had seven children, two of who died in infancy. The names of the other five children are: John, Jr., "Skeet", (died in an accident), Wayne, Allen, Thomas, and James. He has many grandchildren and a "bunch" of great-grandchildren. They also fostered others.

While a prisoner of war, John's faith was his rock. As mentioned earlier, on many occasions while he was being brutally beaten by Japanese guards, he was asked why he didn't die. His response was always the same: "Because God loves me." His faith in God today is at least as strong as it was when he was brutalized.

Master Sargent John Mims

His daily display of faith is a constant inspiration to his family and friends.

After John's retirement, he and Juanita settled down in Hoke County, North Carolina. John suffered the loss of his wife of over fifty-nine years in January 2004.

In 2009, John married his current wife, Nena. She is his helpmate in all things, maintaining his calendar, so he can keep his frequent appointments, and otherwise helping out. The couple now lives in Hoke County near Aberdeen, North Carolina, not very far from Fort Bragg and Camp Mackall. He frequently visits both bases.

John is very active in sharing his experiences as a Japanese prisoner of war to many groups. He frequently visits and speaks to veterans' groups, civic clubs, schools, churches, and just about any group that invites him to tell his story.

A visitor to his home, upon leaving, will probably hear John say, "I love you, and God loves you, and you can't do a thing about it."

John & Nena Mims 2014

References

The following were helpful in writing this book.

Myron B. Pitts, "Death march survivor is a hero on a mission", The Fayetteville Observer, Section B, March 26, 2009

Letter from General Douglas MacArthur's headquarters, January 15, 1942.

Tim Wilkins, "Uncommon Valor, The Moore County Independent, June 30, 2005.

Pat Allen Wilson, "Death March Survivor Marches Again", Life and Leisure, Section B, The News Journal, May 5, 2004

Pat Allen Wilson, "Hoke man keeps Memorial Day alive", Page 1, The News-Journal, May 24, 2006

Hope Myers, "Crawling back from Ward Zero", Paraglide, February 14, 2014

Tom McCallum, "July 5th Freedom Fest to salute military", Richmond County Daily Journal, May 4, 2003

Tom McCallum, "Bataan Death March survivor honors victims", Richmond County Daily Journal, July 4, 2003